INTO
GREEN

Everyday ways to find and lose yourself in nature

Illustrations by
Georgie McAusland

Caro Langton and
Rose Ray of Ro Co

This book is for Lizzy and Will.

Reconnect

14. Set intentions, discover new paths

Wonder

*34. Notice the extraordinary
in the ordinary*

Unlock

*54. Feel the earth,
take root*

Fail

*82. Cultivate chaos,
embrace the accidental*

Reignite

Disappear

Renew

Share

The path that Rose and I took to finding and losing ourselves in green was in no way speedy, conventional or linear, and at times it didn't feel easy.

Back in the mid-noughties, we were graduating from university with that most optimistic of accolades: a fashion design degree. With pink cropped hair, furry jumpers and polka-dot PVC trousers, we descended on London like disco moths; green was the colour of silk swatches, neon lights and cheap beer bottles.

But something kept tugging at us: the sensory lure of gardening and the outdoors. We longed to engage with the spirit of the natural world, so would meet after work and fabricate scenarios that would allow us to connect to nature, design and better wellbeing.

One day, we took the leap and together launched biophilic design studio

Ro Co to help people bring green into their lives. The way we see it, many of us living in cities and towns find ourselves so detached from nature that even when we notice precious glimpses of it, we struggle to really connect. The intensity of urban life can render it messy and exhausting, and green so often becomes the colour of our envy as we stare wistfully at pictures of the lush countryside that other people are enjoying. But when we stop and look, nature is all around us, perhaps especially so in the city, where it grows in spite of manmade obstacles.

Rose and I are not botanists or psychologists (though we know a lot about botany and psychology), but we have experienced firsthand how plants and nature's elements can transform a life, and we want to bring you on the journey that led to us publishing this book.

A note from Caro

WHILE THINKING ABOUT writing this note, I had an 'a-ha!' moment – I realised *Into Green* has a lot to do with confidence, or at least building confidence.

It's about the confidence to unearth identity, and to determine and travel a path that feels authentic. The confidence to believe in an optimistic future. The confidence to hear the voice inside you – it's like an old, forgotten friend – that's willing you to explore your ancient connection to the natural world. And the confidence to honour your failures (and the lessons hiding within them).

Letting go isn't easy. My mind has a tendency to default to chaos, and if this sounds like it would fuel creativity, it hasn't been the case for me – when creating something physical, my hands seem to compensate with freakishly controlled results. I used to give up on projects because what I made never matched what I imagined. In truth, I wrote the chapter Fail because I needed to read it.

In my teenage years and twenties, I thought that anxiety and panic attacks were my body's way of saying I should do less. I turned to nature to soothe myself without realising why – a sort of instinct that told me gardens could alchemise sadness into hope. Now I am older, I know that actually *doing* things helps me understand my feelings far better than sitting and thinking ever could. A garden is a wonderful thing, but *to garden* is more powerful.

No matter what 'into green' means to you, I hope this book inspires confidence and, whenever you have feelings of doubt, stasis or confusion, the ability to answer those with action.

A note from Rose

GREEN WAS THE colour of my childhood. Our higgledy-piggledy family home sat on a plot of rambling countryside that was shared by old badgers and gnarled magnolia trees. I remember roaming the land, running my hands through cocksfoot and Yorkshire fog grasses, collecting seeds, always seeking and amassing trinkets to put in pockets and arrange indoors.

Free afternoons were spent in a hammock underneath a bejewelled cherry tree, the light twinkling through the green canopy. Its resident birds' song would often startle me, exploding with a sound that swelled like an orchestra. There seemed always to be the scent of sap from fir cones and the prickly heat of stinging nettles.

As an adult I longed for a change from this bucolic life, and so settled in cities and towns. My creative spirit was first drawn to fashion and then to set design; the soundtrack to my day became the hum of traffic and the click-click of my computer keyboard.

It usually takes some sort of crisis for us to think about changing our behaviours – for me it was the escalation of the IBS symptoms that I'd suffered most of my adult life, coupled with the pandemic. This perfect storm finally forced me to slow down and reset, and it made me realise I'd become completely detached from my real nature.

So, in some ways, the theme of this book is reconnection. You may not have grown up surrounded by nature, but that doesn't matter. I lost my tether to it for a while, but I found my way back in all kinds of unexpected ways. I can't wait to share them with you.

What 'into green' means to us

ACCORDING TO COLOUR theory, green is the most balanced and calming hue in the spectrum. Sitting right in the middle, it is believed to reduce stress and symbolise stability. For us, green goes hand in hand with feelings of hope, creativity, wonder and a sense of belonging.

'Into green' is about finding a balance: of getting outside to simply enjoy this beautiful planet, as well as using meaningful interactions with nature to cultivate a healthy daily headspace. Before you begin reading, give yourself a moment to think about why you have picked up this book. What are you here to nurture? Is there something standing in your way?

We hope this book can answer some of those questions, and be your guide to improving your experience of urban living. We put emphasis on how you might do this, not why, because you already know that nature is good for you – perhaps you're just struggling to act.

We hope our ideas will excite that urge for positive change, and help you say 'I never thought of it that way.' And we hope they lead you to connect with green so that you can both expand and retreat, grow and disappear and ultimately find and lose yourself in nature.

A note on navigating this book

ORIGINALLY WE DESIGNED this book in two halves: a flipbook with 'finding' at one end and 'losing' at the other. The reader would begin from opposite ends and meet themselves in the middle. Nature helps us find and lose ourselves so comprehensively.

It seemed like a smart idea, but as we tried to execute it, we came to learn that the ways in which each of us interprets nature in order to connect and disconnect are so entwined and nebulous that it was best to let the reader find their own path.

So instead, the themes of *Into Green* flow and merge and intersect from chapter to chapter. If you start at the beginning of the book and read through to the end, you'll find a path that might be fun to follow. Or you could let your mood determine the path for you, and dip in and out, starting and ending with whatever chapter or page grabs you in that moment.

This is your journey, after all.

RECONNECT

*Set intentions,
discover new paths*

You've established that you need more nature in your life, that you are ready to seek out new adventures and sow new seeds, both literally and figuratively. So where to next? How best to direct the connection-seeking, optimistic part of yourself that you've unearthed? What can you do to nurture and nudge that desire?

Should you make a drastic change? Take a foraging course? Keep bees? Find an allotment and plant root vegetables? Go freelance, move to the countryside and start a dahlia farm?

The answer to these questions might be 'heck, yes!'. But grand visions and life-changing leaps that don't quite marry with our daily reality can be a painful reminder of what's out of reach. Some days, the chattering back and forth of our questioning inner voice leaves us glassy eyed and removed from the here and now, as if we've been on the phone to an anxious friend for hours.

What we've found is that real change and connections are forged gently, little by little, with plenty of planning and pauses to let the magic take effect. By treating yourself to some space and time to reconnect, you'll open yourself up to those chance happenings and encounters that help build confidence and cement change.

Nature is all around you, and every chapter here will help you find it. But before you grab your walking boots or secateurs, we'll help you slow down and tune in to yourself so you can channel your energy in the right place and move forward with a clear and focused mind.

By setting intentions and figuring out what might be holding you back, the route forward will clear itself.

Invoke new rituals

OVER THE YEARS, we've found various ways to restore and enrich our relationship with nature, but the thing that's helped us most is redefining what we think of or perceive as 'nature'.

The less you think of nature as something that should be pristine and untouched, and that is perhaps out of reach, then the wider, less expensive and more inclusive it becomes. If you can value small, local scraps of wilderness, you will gift yourself delightful moments of connection. Nature knows no boundaries, and wild is often a state of mind more than a place.

Once the concept of 'nature' changed in our minds, we learned to change our behaviour, too. Below are three good ways to do that.

Make NEW RITUALS to incorporate into your daily routine – these will soon become the habits you can't live without.

Learn new skills through CREATIVE PROJECTS. You'll be amazed how much your confidence progresses by using your hands and sinking into simple processes.

SPARK AWE – because this almost always leads to seeing things differently. Incredible facts, nature's hidden wonders and the science behind why the outdoors is so good for us can be eye-opening. New knowledge is key to positive change.

Throughout this book you'll find these three types of suggestions. Each one is designed to help you set yourself fun challenges and pledges to get to know the natural world better.

As you read, you might mark any suggestions that resonate in a calendar, pushing yourself to try two or three different ones each week or month – do this any way that fits around your life and schedule.

When they come (and they will), celebrate your victories, even the tiniest ones. Celebrate in a way that works for you: do a little dance, make a delicious botanical cocktail, write about it… we know it sounds silly, but who cares? Nature should be joyful, and celebrating even the smallest connection will reinforce why you're making these changes in the first place.

Be empowered by your desire to cultivate your own wildness as well as the planet's. You've got this. You have. Believe it.

Energy

Givers

sunrise wake-ups
morning stretches
warm embraces
stillness
the scent of peppermint
learning something new
dancing leaves
brisk walks
smiles at strangers
the shimmer of a spider's web
gasps of cold air
time alone
aerial views
kind words
trusting your instincts
the bold leap of a squirrel
stargazing
clear boundaries
moonlit strolls
sunlight dancing on walls

Build confidence with a journal

EXTERNALISING IDEAS, thoughts and daily happenings on paper has really helped us to better understand ourselves and find our flow. As the songwriter Nick Cave pointed out, we should 'write things down, in order to advance the idea, as this indicates a readiness to receive'.

The process of writing down thoughts and ideas not only helps to clarify them, but by keeping track of plans and observations, we can inadvertently seed our desires on the page and watch them flourish as we find the confidence to take action. Think of it like sowing seed and cultivating a garden – a tiny garden made of paper you can keep in your pocket.

Keeping a journal can inspire you to take the leap from imagining change to making it real. Here are some ideas to get you started...

Start by writing down what you long for. List places you'd like to explore, plants that ignite your senses and quotes that give you goosebumps. Stick in projects torn from magazines and anything else that sparks your creativity, interest or goals. Seeing these things together will help your plans take form.

Track the progress of some seedlings and observe how their growth makes you feel. Celebrate the successes of your experiments and allow the failures to fuel your curiosity. Over time, the filled pages will begin to help you make sense of what success means to you, and most importantly, help you to work out how to achieve it.

Journalling can help you better understand the seasons of yourself: how your energy levels change depending on the time of day, month and year. You might find that the first hour of a Sunday morning is when your ideas are sharpest, right after a long walk, or that you like multitasking, making muddy notes while your hands are covered in earth. When you understand yourself at your best, it will help you find joy.

Try adding little symbols or number ratings on each entry in your journal to help you identify patterns. For example, you might find a connection between how many hours you spent gardening that day and your mood on a scale of 0 to 9. If you menstruate and feel your energy or mood influenced by this, you could note the day of your cycle and see if a certain phase is your most productive.

Keep your journal private and remember the format is entirely up to you.

'Craft is the
hard work.
Connection the
reward'

KAE TEMPEST,
ON CONNECTION

Burn and bury

Conjure a clear path ahead by releasing captive thoughts with the support of fire and earth.

On a new or full moon, jot down any regrets or worries on paper; remember that no one else will ever read them.

Hold the paper tightly between your palms and imagine yourself releasing those thoughts into the air with a couple of big breaths.

Then take the paper outside and burn it inside a fireproof pot. As it burns, imagine the licking flames and smoke banishing any negative energy into the ether.

Once cooled, take the ashes and bury them in earth. If you don't have a place to do this, simply blow them away. Visualise your new intentions and vow to take a confident step forward.

Nurture breath

THERE IS NO right way to meditate, but there are plenty of reasons to bring your version of the practice into your weekly routine.

Many of us deal with daily stressors that trigger short and subconsciously held breaths. This has a knock-on effect on the processes of your body. From physical growth and cognition to healthy sleep and digestion, oxygen is essential.

When you feel disconnected from the physical, meditation will help you to breathe better and bring awareness back to your body, encouraging you to connect to its natural rhythm through moments of stillness and focus. This increased awareness will supercharge your senses, giving you the clarity to notice what's going on in (and outside of) your body and mind.

The breathing and walking meditations on the following pages can be practised outdoors in a garden, park or woodland, or indoors, wherever you are. Try them when you need a moment to relax or find yourself in a setting that you'd like to deeply connect to.

Breathe as you are

Find a natural position – standing, sitting or reclining – that feels comfortable. Feel the weight of your body supported beneath you. Rest your right hand on your belly and your left hand on your chest – your diaphragm should sit between your two palms. Soften your gaze or close your eyes.

Take a slow, long breath in through your nose and feel your belly expand beneath your right hand. Exhale slowly and fully through your nose and feel your belly fall. Try to keep your left hand from rising and falling. Continue to take deep breaths like this for five minutes or so.

Don't worry if your mind wanders, just bring your attention back to the physical sensation of your breath and your body rising and falling like a tide.

With regular practice, you'll find that your breath will become more full outside of your meditations and you will be able to practise meditating for longer periods of time.

Ramble in rhythm

Take yourself out on a stroll without worrying about the destination. Become aware of the weight and fluidity of your body, and fall into a pace that feels natural and comfortable.

Using the slow breathing you have practised, together with the gentle rhythm of your gait, allow your breath and step to create an easy and consistent partnership. Tune into your surroundings to ground yourself in the now.

You might notice distinct sounds near and far, or shades of colour and texture in the trees and sky. You might feel the sunshine on your skin or the wind passing around your body and face. The goal is to recognise and acknowledge the sensations without dwelling on them.

Whenever thoughts stray, keep tuning in to the rhythm of your feet meeting the ground. You'll be surprised by how much you notice when you teach yourself to stay present in this way.

Square breathing is an easy way to connect with your breath and to notice how you feel in this moment. Using the outside of the square as part of the meditation, slowly draw your finger around the shape's outline as you breathe deeply. Try doing this three or four times.

Simple yet strangely hypnotic.

breathe in ———————→

hold

hold

breathe out ←———————

WONDER

*Notice the extraordinary
in the ordinary*

If the year 2020 taught us anything, it's that small pleasures are powerful. Faced with the prospect of staying local, with no clear route ahead, we had to adapt almost overnight in order to find joy in the ordinary and the familiar.

At first it seemed like it might be harder than ever to explore the wilderness. Those of us with no garden questioned how we could find solace in nature when we weren't allowed outside more than once a day (if at all).

But something unexpected happened: people began to realise how genuinely they valued nature and they sought it out in new ways. Rose, on her daily loop around Margate on the coast of England, began noticing details with a new clarity: seagulls nesting in the chalky cliffs, kicking translucent shells from their nests; sea daisies with yellow yolk centres and delicate petals shivering in the breeze.

I embraced the challenge to think big in a small living space, and grew English curly parsley, Thai basil and scented sweet peas from seed to adorn my doorstep. With no private outside space to relax in, that step became a defiant little slice of garden that slowly spilled out on to the pavement.

It seems people everywhere were rediscovering their inner curiosity and noticing the charming little tuft of wild poppies in the supermarket car park, or the moss carpeting the brick walls of front gardens. Suddenly, nature was everywhere, in full, spirit-lifting colour.

In this section we celebrate those small discoveries, sharing our observations and tips on how to find beauty in the seemingly mundane.

Seeing things differently

HAVE YOU EVER noticed that when you learn the name of a plant or bird or butterfly, it immediately begins popping up in unexpected places? It can feel as if the universe is giving you a wink.

But as busy adults, we're often distracted, have no time to stop; we override our natural desires to be curious and spontaneous with a need for efficiency. We tend to walk the shortest route on autopilot, and so the small, everyday moments of joy the natural world offers can pass us by.

Ask the universe to surprise you. Step out of your front door embodying a new perspective, a sort of more observant alter ego. You might imagine you're a fresh-eyed tourist or a keen botanist. What would they notice and value? Which element would they want to look closer at?

Quieten distraction: ditch your headphones, put off making that call and avoid the temptation to multitask. Remember to look up. The details that spark and hold your attention – especially observations that perhaps other people seem oblivious to – are fuel for your own unique point of view.

Make a daily stroll a new ritual: it's one of the simplest ways to forge a personal connection to local wildlife and notice the subtle shift in the seasons. The natural world offers so many small, uplifting moments. Collect them, learn more about them, and the universe will keep giving you more.

Taste your neighbourhood

WE LEARNT THE hard way that when you give a child a flower, they presume it's edible. When we ran our market stall in east London, a child snatched a bristly mini cactus and tried to eat it – luckily her mother noticed just in time.

Rose was the same as a child, and quickly learned to forage. She grew up hunting edible treasures in the rambling woodland that cushioned her countryside home: giant puffball mushrooms, handfuls of jewel-like wild strawberries, knobbly gooseberries and sweet-tart blackberries.

When she left home to work in London, she gradually forgot to look. Anyone who has rented in a busy city or town knows that feeling of disconnection, that lack of belonging and attachment to a place. Getting hands-on with the flora in your local neighbourhood can feel, well, a bit unnatural.

But during the pandemic, the enforced slowness and geographical restriction helped Rose reignite her forager's vision, turning her hometown of Margate on the Kent coast into an edible landscape.

She began hunting seaweed (it's almost never poisonous) and spotting dulse (*Palmaria palmata*) growing around tidal pools, its long, leathery, mahogany tendrils shiny from the sea. On walks along the coast from Pegwell Bay to Kingsdown Beach she saw pops of colour in the muted shingle marking seeds blown wild from neighbouring gardens. Taking the time to get closer, she discovered fennel, red hot pokers and sea kale, with its turquoise plumes of frilly leaves.

She found that by foraging – which invariably meant using her hands, working at identification and taking treasures home – she felt closer to the landscape around her. She would notice the soft texture of a plant's leaves and the fragrant smell it left on her fingertips, and down in the sand she could spy on creatures that would never have been seen had she been striding along the promenade. These off-track explorations helped calm her anxieties and deepen her connection to the local land.

Invest in a short course or a foraging guide that's specific to your part of the world. Learning how to forage and find edible wonders safely and responsibly helps to build confidence when getting up close to your local free food. From whelks on the beach to pockets of urban green bursting with wildflowers, there are treasures in the streets, parks and woodland all around.

Edible urban flora

1.

2.

3.

1. ELDERBERRY
Sambucus

The flowers and ripe berries (cooked)
are edible, but avoid leaves and stems

2. DANDELION
Taraxacum officinale

3. MAGNOLIA
Magnolia grandiflora

Mild citrus-ginger-cardamom blossoms
can be pickled or added to a salad

4. WILD GARLIC
Allium ursinum

Enjoy leaves, buds, seedheads and bulbs

5. STINGING NETTLE
Urtica dioica

6. HONEYSUCKLE
Lonicera

Harvest blossoms and nectar for iced tea

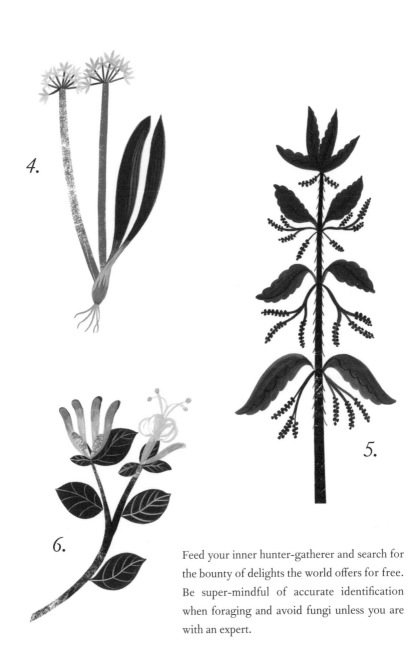

4.

5.

6.

Feed your inner hunter-gatherer and search for the bounty of delights the world offers for free. Be super-mindful of accurate identification when foraging and avoid fungi unless you are with an expert.

Spark

Wonder

look through a telescope
eat edible flowers
follow the moon
fill a bird feeder
take a foraging course
make dandelion root coffee
look for fractals in the universe
get down on your hands and knees
draw a tree and frame the picture
find a tree with a chorus of bird song
stare into the depths of an agate crystal
have a picnic under the canopy of a tree
pick up a rock and use it as an incense holder
slice a fruit in half, marvel at the cross-section
leave a foraged flower between the pages of an old book
learn the name of a cloud formation and find it in the sky
buy a film camera and make nature your muse
study a snowflake, there are no two the same
look out for a murmuration at dusk
walk in synchrony with a friend
identify a constellation of stars
befriend a beekeeper
tip your hat to an urban fox

A world within a flower

IF YOU WANT to see a world within a flower then buy yourself a romanesco broccoli. Remarkably beautiful, this brassica is made up of psychedelic spirals called fractals, which when viewed up close mirror the structure of the vegetable as a whole. They're a mathematical marvel, a brilliant contrast to the soil each bright green head blooms from.

Life gets even more astounding when you look at it magnified: a spot of fungi becomes an otherworldly landscape; a seed becomes an impossibly complex sculpture; a cross-section of a bamboo stem looks freakishly like a pattern of monkey faces. Insect wings magnified are so glorious they're hard to describe.

From coiled shells and succulents like the *Aloe polyphylla* to pinecones and pineapples, natural spirals of the Fibonacci sequence – a series of numbers in which each number is the sum of the two preceding it – can be seen hiding in abundance amongst organic forms.

The closer you look, the more you slow down and the smaller you might feel yourself. The world is enormous and magnificent, full of unbelievably extraordinary things, and looking at it up close can make us feel lucky to be part of it.

Enhance your vision with a botanical loupe (a neat, foldable magnifying lens) to see the magnificent details of nature's forms with crystal clarity. If you can't move your subject up to you, don't be afraid to get down on your hands and knees: once any onlookers realise you haven't collapsed, you'll only inspire their awe too, we promise.

Before photography existed, people would press botanical specimens to classify and preserve their extraordinary characteristics. Create your own herbarium by pressing wildflowers you admire between the pages of a heavy book for a couple of weeks. Pick a warm spot, as the faster the flower dries, the more colour will be preserved. You might leave the flower there to spark some future reader's imagination or just marvel at the intricacy of its construction and individual character.

'People from
a planet without
flowers would
think we must be
mad with joy
the whole time
to have such things
about us'

IRIS MURDOCH

Draw from nature

IF YOU WANT to forge a deeper connection with nature, try drawing it. Drawing forces us to stop and really *look*. It helps us to see what's around us.

So often as adults we look at a landscape with a wide-angle gaze, and when we try to capture it in a photograph, the convenience and speed of a smartphone can stop us experiencing it for ourselves.

Drawing helps us to narrow our focus and appreciate the extraordinary details that are often overlooked or even more interesting than the entire scene. All you need is a pencil and paper. It is a calming activity, improves brain function, creativity and releases dopamine which makes us buzz with happiness. In one German study, researchers found that making art activated brain connectivity and helped build psychological resilience – something we all need. Put simply, drawing is a satisfying rest from all the anxious thinking our frazzled brains do.

And plants make effortlessly captivating subjects throughout the year: riotous wildflowers, sculptural houseplants like calatheas and monsteras, skeletal trees in winter. Plants ignite the imagination and help creativity flow.

To draw from nature, first set your scene: you might simply sit in front of a houseplant at home or seek out a tree in the wilderness. Don't worry about technique as you start to make marks on the paper, lose yourself in the exploration of line to find your creative rhythm.

Set yourself time-restricted challenges of 1, 5 and 10 minutes and use these techniques to get started:

—— Draw with your less dominant hand: it will feel a little uncomfortable at first, but the results are wonderfully surreal.

—— Draw without release: imagine your pen is a magnet clamped to the page and don't lift it off the sheet for the duration of the drawing.

—— Draw without peeking: practice your skills of observing closely and survey the scene for 1 minute. Now draw the scene without looking up from the page.

—— Draw from touch: close your eyes and use the surprisingly acute perception of your fingertips to explore an organic form like a dried leaf, shell or pinecone. Without looking at the page, try drawing what you felt. It sounds a bit strange, but we've created unexpectedly kooky pieces this way.

When you stop

you start to see

When you see you
start to look

When you look
you become
curious

When you become
curious you
start to feel

all the

wonder in

the world

in

yourself

UNLOCK

*Feel the earth,
take root*

In good times and bad, few things can imbue life with joy and hope quite like gardening.

When we've messed things up at work, said something thoughtless to a friend, screeched at a sibling or disappointed the dog (again), it can be hard to get out of a negative groove. Sowing seeds and nurturing new growth can be potent antidotes to that out-of-sync feeling, taking us from being at odds with the flow of the universe to riding the wave once more.

Even the simple act of weeding or turning earth with bare hands is enough to turn a bad day into a great one. The pure physicality of it – the damp, fecund aromas, the dirt-caked fingernails, the slightly achy back – is such a contrast to the sterile realities of urban life, and a reminder to move forwards with optimism and purpose.

Perhaps your desire to get hands-on and garden is urgent. It could be a small voice inside your head that constantly whispers: take me outside, you know it'll be good for you. Maybe you long to be surrounded by the plants you have yet to sow or to take pride in the harvest you have yet to plan. You imagine smiling as you chop up the carrot you grew, or identifying bird song or wildflowers as you potter outside.

Most of us are certain of how profoundly this would enrich our lives, but we struggle to start. We know the feeling, and want to help you turn any unearthed doubts into action.

The following pages not only explore how gardening is a way to invest in your future happiness, they also offer straightforward suggestions on how to start small and find your flow.

Start a garden.
Start a garden because it's a magical thing.
Start right where you are, whether your sunny patch of possibility
is a quarter of an acre or a small punnet on a windowsill.

Start a garden in your mind's eye, no matter
where you are. Imagine vines wound around
trellises, leaves that cascade, flowers that bloom at
unanticipated times, a place filled with smells that
call creatures from far and wide to find their way
to you and tend your garden by your side. Start a
garden with a pencil and a piece of paper torn from a
notepad. Draw a picture of the view from a window
of what your garden might look like in July. Draw
an outline of the beds in your veg patch, one for each
plant family you want to taste, and imagine yourself
five or seven years from now, poised to start the
rotation again.

Start a garden and call it a garden even if it's only humble and not
yet full of plants. Start a garden because, soon enough, you will see a
beautiful and unexpected insect that you've never met before and you
can introduce yourselves to each other. Start a garden and think through
your worries there, while picking tomatoes or smelling jasmine or
pulling weeds.

Start a garden with someone you love. Shovelling a ton of compost is easier with a friend. Tell them about your triumphs and troubles while you harvest beans into the same basket.

Start a garden if, like me, you were taught to believe in something bigger than yourself.

Start a garden because there's nothing quite like it to gesture to the universe that you have faith in the future and you want to be part of making it a bit more beautiful and delicious and abundant.

BY CLAIRE RATINON

Set your headspace

ONE POWERFUL THING that makes an allotment or a garden so enticing is the act of taking ownership of a defined space. Knowing that this plot is your responsibility, and having physical boundaries for your planting experiments, can be a thrilling challenge. It's as if that set place welcomes a new headspace, a new you.

So the first thing we'd recommend doing is figuring out specifically where you'll channel your energy. Stake claim to one bright spot and make a promise to transform it. It's great to start small, so don't worry if you don't have a garden: an indoor shelf in the living room, a tiny balcony with enough space to hang a box over the railing, a front doorstep or a windowsill all make perfect horticultural playgrounds. See if you can identify a place that receives six to eight hours of sunlight a day and that's shielded from the wind – then make it yours.

Take a photo of the place you've chosen in its current empty state (because we all love a before-and-after shot!) and see if framing it through a lens helps you visualise the planting design.

From that point on, imagine your progress like a dial. No matter how complex the project, as long as you've turned the dial one degree in the right direction every day, you've succeeded. That might mean researching plants you like online, visiting a garden centre or starting a compost heap. It could mean germinating a single, pink, capsule-shaped mango seed, rotating your rubber plant or plucking a few dead leaves from some fading basil. When you put less pressure on yourself, you'll find each tiny task leads naturally to the next and before you know it you'll be happily lost in the process. Essentially, you're boosting motivation and relieving creative pressure by breaking the end goal down into manageable steps, and freeing your imagination so you can find an expansive way of thinking.

To get started, how about creating an edible window box? Sowed in the spring, salad seeds like radish, lettuce and spring onion will germinate so quickly that you'll be harvesting a crop in a month or two. If you go on to find a space in a communal garden or have your own, a raised bed is the perfect place to transplant young edibles and expand your crop (see page 178).

Or go bigger! Potatoes and tomatoes will grow in a large pot on a sunny doorstep. Lavender, thyme and single-flowered species of bedding plants like lobelia, diascia and verbena will love living in a hanging basket and give you an instant hit of joy when you walk through your front door. They'll also support bees, butterflies and other valuable pollinators.

If this sounds overwhelming, forget the plants for a minute and have fun hunting for the container itself. Unlike plants, the container can't die, so this is your chance to be creative, colourful, spontaneous. Just make sure it has drainage holes, or, if not, that you can drill some in.

'My garden's boundaries are the horizon'

DEREK JARMAN

Houseplants hold the key

I ONCE DATED someone – let's call him Colin, since he mentioned he liked caterpillars – who confided in me his private oath not to seek out a girlfriend until he'd managed to keep a potted aloe vera plant alive for a year. 'I transcended my ego,' he said, leaning in self-importantly while I gulped my wine, 'so that I could nurture something that longed for my care, but not smother it. You see, I have a tendency to love things *too* much.' I smiled nervously and eyeballed the door. It was a metaphor for the complexities of a woman, Colin clarified, mistaking my stunned silence for awe.

We never met again. I sort of knew what he meant, though.

Houseplants are like pets. They rely on us and mirror our basic needs: hydration, fresh air, stability, sunlight, physical touch. But we are also connected to them. You may become as emotionally dependent on your towering fiddle-leaf fig as you are on a dear friend. You might murmur encouragement to freshly propagated philodendron cuttings, stroking each glossy, unfurling tendril. You probably wonder regularly if your monstera's hungry roots need room to spread or if they are lonely. Reader, you'll find no judgment here.

It's easy to shower overbearing affection on fuzzy, rootless air plants or throw our arms crushingly around a gorgeous clivia when it blooms in a shock of tangerine trumpets, but (most of the time) we can rein that urge in, knowing instinctively how to care for our houseplants so they thrive rather than fatally succumb to our love.

With many of us having no outside space to play in, a motley crew of cacti, succulents and tropical plants can become our own miniature garden to get lost in. If you are one such houseplant lover, acknowledge your ability, give yourself credit for keeping your plants happy, and let them build your confidence in order to move in a new direction.

For us, our houseplant gang opened up a new path – a sort of less-intimidating side door – into the equally magical world of growing edibles and flowering garden plants. Things like root vegetables, nasturtiums, lettuce and tomatoes ask for about the same level of attention as a tropical houseplant, and offer so much in return. Just imagine how wonderful it would be to let houseplants introduce you to a whole other world of gardening.

For those of us who like to carefully plot and plan before taking action, the endless possibilities of gardening can feel as overwhelming as they are exciting. You might find yourself stalled by countless planting options, conflicting plant-care considerations or even the sheer variety of seeds or species you'd like to investigate. These early distractions – and the fear of wasting precious materials – can sometimes hold us back from taking that first step outside, trowel confidently in hand. Release the pressure by taking stock of your ideas and plans by writing them down – treat your journal like a second brain, a place to store knowledge, mark reminders and work out what the best first step might be. Writing down your observations will naturally clear space for better focus and encourage action.

Branch out and grow

So you love houseplants? Use your favourite as a jump-off point to explore the world of edibles and flowers

1.	2.
A STRIPY *TRADESCANTIA ZEBRINA*	A LUSH AND TROPICAL TERRARIUM
Potted lavender, basil and thyme	Edible microgreens on a kitchen windowsill
Sea holly *Eryngium × zabelii*, calendula and cosmos in a sunny patch	A collection of flowering, scented pelargoniums for indoors and out

3.	4.	5.
A BEGONIA	AN ASPARAGUS FERN	A PONYTAIL PALM
↓	↓	↓
A pot of marigolds	Spinach, rocket and leafy lettuce in a window box	A tomato plant or scented sweet peas on your doorstep
↓	↓	↓
Carrots, radishes and leafy lettuce in a chunky container	A cut-flower patch of snapdragons, pretty scabious and fragrant phlox	A hanging basket of coleus, trailing geraniums and nasturtium

The universe underfoot

THE COMPLEXITY OF life that's in (and supported by) the earth beneath our feet is incredible, and the more we find out about it, the more we feel a need to be near it.

Soil stores carbon, filters water and provides anchorage for roots, not to mention nutrients and oxygen. It is so vitally biodiverse that in one teaspoon you might find billions of microorganisms, and in certain parts of the world, you can encounter soil that is billions of years old.

The dazzling squadron of unsung heroes living in soil is endless, and they each play a role in plant growth and nutrient cycling. There are worms, invertebrates, microbes, larvae, algae and tardigrades (these are eight-legged micro-animals otherwise known as moss piglets or water bears and they are so tough they can survive frozen and boiling temperatures and extreme radiation, and can even procreate in deep-sea water and outer space). There are also vast webs of fungal threads called mycelia, which trade nutrients with plants in return for the sugars they need to thrive.

And you know that soothing scent of freshly turned garden earth or forest air? It's not in your head: it's partly due to a protein called geosmin which is released by bacteria and fungi. Humans are extremely sensitive to the chemical's scent and our ability to perceive it as a sign of healthy soil ties in with our ancient bond to the land. You can taste geosmin, too – higher levels of it in freshly grown vegetables give them their earthy flavour.

Soil is full of healthy bacteria that can support your gut's microbiome when you breathe in its tiny particles. There's also a bacterium called 'mycobacterium' that is thought to balance serotonin levels in the brain. We can even make medicine from soil: microorganisms discovered underground have yielded antibiotics that can fight fierce pathogens otherwise resistant to other drugs. The reasons to get closer to soil go on and on.

Much of the land underfoot is still a mystery, but its qualities are there to help you thrive. There's a universe full of untapped potential down there, and you are very much bound to it. As Margaret Atwood wisely said: 'In the spring, at the end of the day, you should smell like dirt.'

When it comes to buying compost, always look for peat-free products. The same goes when buying houseplants, which are often grown in a medium containing peat. Peat comes from the decomposed remains of a valuable species of moss called sphagnum moss, and is one of the world's most important carbon stores. Peat is mined from bogs for use in the gardening industry, and is not a renewable resource since it takes centuries to form.

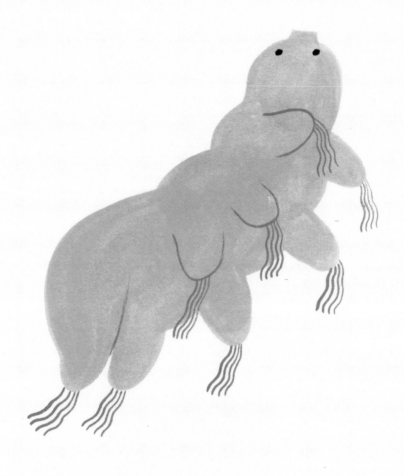

Be more tardigrade.

Boost yourself with bulbs

It's easy to see how planting bulbs in autumn becomes an annual ritual for gardeners – it not only gets you outdoors during autumn's shortening days, but all that anticipation of the flowers to come, and thinking ahead to spring, are real mood-boosters.

It works well to grow a mix of spring-flowering bulbs in a container. Look for paperwhites (*Narcissus papyraceus*), crocus, tulip, daffodil or hyacinth bulbs which can be planted in a terracotta plant pot (just make sure the container is no less than 40cm deep and allows good drainage).

Start with a layer of multipurpose compost at the bottom (make sure it's at least 5–10cm deep) and your biggest bulb. The idea is to create alternate layers of bulbs and compost, going from the largest bulb at the bottom to the smallest on top. You want to plant each bulb at a depth of at least three times its size and push it in pointy side up. You can plant them close together, but make sure they don't touch.

To bring life to the pot while you wait for spring, plant the top layer with bedding plug plants like pansies or primrose. These can be removed once they die back to make space for the bulbs to flower. Protect the pot from frost and keep the soil moist if it hasn't rained for a while.

Pot with purpose

NURTURING PLANTS FROM seed is pure joy. It's like germinating your own positivity: tucking dry seeds into the earth and watching each bright stem and tiny leaf establish under your care is a wonderfully visual way to spark hope, no matter life's challenges.

With a bit of planning, it can be easy to plant up your own garden in a pot. The following pages show three planting combinations to inspire you, and all the plants listed will support valuable wildlife on your windowsill or doorstep. But there are so many beautiful, low-maintenance options that you might find a completely different combination to suit your taste.

A wildflower meadow in a pot might sound ambitious, but it's totally possible, and wildflowers like poppies, cornflower, camomile and forget-me-nots are natural mood-lifters. They don't ask for much care and will self-seed season after season.

Creating a pot or patch with medicinal or herbal tea plants is an equally low-maintenance enterprise. Adding a fresh element to healing hot drinks and other recipes is a way to bring nature into your everyday habits.

Planting a sensory garden is like growing your own private moment of calm. Once your plants are growing, you can rub the leaves between your fingers and breathe in the fragrances with slow breaths.

Pot with purpose

*Create a lush, mini-garden to add a new sensory
dimension to your doorstep or windowsill*

1. CHOOSE YOUR GROWING SPACE	2. ADD DRAINAGE	3. PICK YOUR DESIGN	4. SOIL
Terracotta pot	Pebbles	Wildflower garden *Resilience, spontaneity, delight*	Organic peat-free compost, plus seedling compost for top 2cm
Window box	Used and washed-out coffee filters	Herbal tea garden *Stimulation, verve, potential*	Organic peat-free compost
Patch of land	Broken terracotta		
Hanging basket	Broken ceramics	Sensory garden *Memory, intention, reconnection*	Organic peat-free compost
Antique planter			
Veg patch edges			

5. PLANT COMBINATIONS	6. METHOD	7. GROWING	8. CARE
Annual mixed wildflower seed suitable for container gardening	Scatter seeds and cover with a sprinkling of seedling compost during the spring	Plants will flower over the summer	Keep soil moist. Prolong flowering by deadheading throughout summer
Lemon balm Chamomile Moroccan mint Common sage	Easiest to plant as plug plants in spring Space 5cm apart	Harvest flowers in the mornings To harvest leaves, pick the top 2-4cm just above a pair of new leaves during the growing season	Keep soil moist. Bring herbs indoors over winter to avoid frosts or wrap in horticultural fleece to keep them protected
Strawberry Borage Scented-leaf pelargonium Nasturtium	Easiest to plant as plug plants in spring Space 5cm apart	Strawberries grow better in large pots but still provide a crop in small spaces. Choose varieties of scented and edible pelargoniums – rub the leaves for fragrance and infuse in cordials. Nasturtiums flowers and leaves are edible, and peppery	Keep soil moist. Prolong flowering by deadheading. Prune fast-growing borage back by half in mid-summer. Nasturtium, pelargonium and borage are good companion plants to strawberries as they deter insects from the fruit

Now be like a worm

and get a wiggle on.

FAIL

Cultivate chaos,
embrace the accidental

Being creative isn't easy. Failing is. At least, that's how you might feel when you begin to act on your desire to nurture and grow plants. Ingrained fears of doing things badly can crop up when experiments go wrong, or even put you off trying in the first place.

The truth is, learning to be more adventurous – and daring to lean into the often unpromising results – requires a willingness to fail, possibly even to receive criticism. That might not come naturally at first. Like us, you might hesitate to take risks, the hangover of an education that taught uniformity, competition and, above all, excellence. The value of failure and its connection to real wellbeing is a notion we might be lucky enough to explore only much later, as adults.

Any new venture – be it as ambitious as adopting an allotment or as simple as a taking a daily walk – is bound to have its false starts and bumpy moments, so to begin you need to be kind enough to let yourself fail, even if it's just a little.

But how can we learn to relinquish control and trust that everything will be okay? And if we do slip up, what can we do to embrace messiness and keep up morale? In this chapter we'll explore some of the reasons you might be holding yourself back, the many ways nature can inspire us to let go and suggestions for how to shake off your worries so you can unearth your potential to grow badly in order to grow better.

Because what we've learnt is that by collaborating with the natural world, rather than trying to control it, you'll not only embrace your creative spirit, you'll find you can become fearless, too.

Explore the shadows

I BECAME MY grandma's housemate after Rose and I graduated and both moved to London. Ann was a child of World War II and she fully embodied the 'make do and mend' spirit; she was unshakeably resourceful and a master of improvisation. In her eyes, every little worn or torn thing was worth something. If you had an idea, you didn't dawdle, you took action... and you stuck at it. I delighted in her vision, which was so at odds with my generation's throwaway culture.

When she passed away, I resolved that nothing in her house would go to waste. Determined to find a new home for every battered utensil and book, I discovered an old journal in her study, fat with glossy photographs and diary-style entries recording the allotment she had shared with her best friend, Cicely. In it they had mapped out their seasonal planting experiments, adding follow-up notes detailing in tiny writing their failures and successes.

The review of their spring-summer 1996 crop read like a tragedy: raspberries were 'ravaged by squirrels', sprouting broccoli was 'lost to white fly', tomatoes were 'scorched in frost', onions were 'very good but stolen!', sweetcorn was 'disappointing', as too were the transplanted lettuces. Other varieties simply 'all died'. I couldn't help but laugh when I read each effort's verdict, probably – like all of her creations – far too harshly critiqued. The photos of my grandma and Cicely grinning, thrusting forks into soil and surrounded by showers of potatoes, told a different story.

There's a scribble on the border of the map of the apparently disastrous plot that reads: 'beautiful self-seeded mystery flower'. And I think that is just about the best analogy for what happens when you lose yourself in a passion project and stay open to the unintentional. The benefits aren't obvious; they spring up by accident. Suddenly, out of the shambles of a new idea, something wonderful shows itself, worthy of your attention.

My point is, your next great idea is hiding somewhere amongst the dead, the disappointing and the stolen. One day, after many more days of gruelling hard work, it appears half-hidden in the shadows: a beautiful self-seeded mystery flower.

Preserve the seasons

If you long to bring nature indoors but are failing to keep plants alive (trust us, you're not alone), let dried plants and flowers become your thing. Many hold on to their scent and colour, and will look beautiful for years. Our favourites are yellow craspedia, ranunculus, globe amaranth, purple statice and grasses such as canary, feather and pampas.

You can easily air-dry fresh bouquets by hanging stems upside down for a couple of weeks in a warm spot away from direct sunlight (which can bleach their colour).

'Invention, it must
be humbly admitted,
does not consist
in creating out of void
but out of chaos'

MARY SHELLEY

Find beauty in chaos

THERE WILL COME a point in the next creative pursuit you stick at – be it planting wildflowers, designing a patchwork quilt, styling a plant shelf in your living room or even writing a book – when the elements you have joined together will take on a life of their own.

You can't force it, you'll just recognise the moment right after it happens. In a flash, you'll find yourself swept up by some unstoppable current: you are on to something great.

This rare moment is luminous; it's at the core of creative spirit. The writer Maria Popova describes this 'immersive, elated intimacy with the work' as the exact point that 'you get out of your own way'.

But an ingrained pursuit of perfection might hold you back from getting there. Many cultures have an obsession with boundaries and order – just look at the rows of neatly razed lawns around you. Losing control tends to be seen as either an indulgence or something shameful.

This kind of total order is an act of self-sabotage, invented to hide the irregularity of our nature. It is disorder – accidents, random mutations, coincidence – that gives life space to thrive.

'If everything existed in uniformity, the gravity that created the stars and planets would not exist,' remarked the theorist and poet Brianna Wiest. 'Without breaks, faults and gaps, nothing could grow and nothing could become.'

When you need to loosen up your creative spirit, collaborating with the aesthetics and energy of the seasons will remind you of the value of cyclical growth and adaptation. Nature teaches us the joys of abundance, of beauty in chaos. It also reassures us that positive things grow from the void.

The musician and artist Brian Eno, whose process is so inspired by the random and uncontrollable, once said: 'The tiniest seed in the right situation turns into the most beautiful forest. And then the most promising seed in the wrong situation turns into nothing.' Perhaps he meant the right situation is one that is open, responsive and unafraid, not trying to control but to gently nurture and see where that leads.

Give your seeds the right situation, both metaphorically and literally. That might mean learning a new skill, which can only be a positive thing, because it's often when we are in that wonderfully amateur stage that we're our most expressive and original, less affected by thoughts of quality or merit.

It's natural to make mistakes in the beginning, and creating something that matches what you imagine isn't easy. But remember, 'right' and 'normal' don't really exist. Bold choices, beautiful things and a better sense of our true selves come from welcoming the unexpected, embracing change and remaining open – it's what creativity is all about.

After pruning weeds like daisies, knapweeds and dandelions, shake them over a sheet of plastic to collect any seeds that drop. Mix the seeds with some wet soil and roll into little balls. Squash the mini-seed bombs into the cracks in your walls or paving to let the wildflowers soften manmade edges.

Embrace any inevitable gardening disasters by sharing spectacular fails with a green-fingered ally. It might be a tray of seeds that didn't germinate or lettuces gobbled by slugs. Send an unflattering photo with a descriptive caption – declare the loss with gusto and laugh together at the absurdity of trying to control nature. Then make compost, and let your mishap foster another try.

Garden

with
Abandon

Elevate the most peculiar element
Arrange alphabetically
Bring your least favourite to the front
What would the person you most admire do?
Merge the boundaries
Add five more
Treat the oldest part to something new
Look at it sideways
Champion your wildness
Feel it with your eyes closed
Emphasise opposites
Silent scream
What would amazingly awful look like?
Come back to it later
Explain your idea to a child
It could always smell better
Look closer
Let the rebellious one be

Bundle dyeing with food waste

BUNDLE DYEING ASKS you to embrace the unexpected and rewards you with beautifully coloured fabrics that prove just how pleasing it can be to surrender control. It's a fairly simple technique that involves transferring the natural colour from plant material on to cloth to create a random series of marks and stains akin to tie-dyeing.

This sort of natural dyeing works best with organic, unbleached cotton or linen (since it doesn't contain any factory nasties) or light-coloured silk, wool, bamboo or tencel. You can experiment with anything that needs cheering up, such as silk scarfs, bed covers, tea towels or tote bags.

Create your own colour palette using compostable kitchen leftovers like avocado pits and skins, onion skins, turmeric, pomegranate seeds and skins, beetroot, coffee, tea bags, dry marigold flowers, carrot tops, rosemary, acacia powder, hibiscus tea… the list goes on! You can also root around in the wild or the garden to collect fresh petals, leaves, berries and stems to add colour and shapes to your dyed fabric. You might choose those from a place that has meaning or feels special to you.

The satisfaction of seeing each uniquely dyed creation you make dancing in the breeze on your clothes line is the most heart-lifting feeling. Each pattern and colour will tell a story of the world around you and your connection to it.

BUNDLE DYEING WITH FOOD WASTE

Natural dyes respond best to natural fabrics, such as raw cotton, linen and silk. This project works beautifully with plain linen napkins, a silk cami or cotton tablecloth. Always use separate pots and tools for dyeing to avoid contamination with your kitchen equipment. Open your windows wide for ventilation. And always boil berries or foraged plants outside to avoid breathing in fumes.

FIND YOURSELF:
—— Fabric
—— Gloves, face mask, goggles
—— Large stainless steel pot for simmering and steaming
—— Alum powder (use 8% of the weight of your material)
—— Plastic sheet
—— Light-coloured vinegar (apple or white wine) in a spray bottle
—— Plant materials
—— Rubber band or a length of string
—— Tongs for turning the bundle

I. Wear gloves, face mask and eye protection when working with the alum. Place the alum in the pot together with enough water to cover your fabric. Add the fabric and simmer over a low heat for 60 minutes in a well-ventilated area.

2. When cool, remove and squeeze the water from the fabric. Remove any excess water by placing it in a washing machine on the spin setting.

3. Protect your floor or surface with a plastic sheet, then lay the damp fabric on top, smoothing out any wrinkles for a flat surface.

4. Liberally spray the fabric with vinegar.

5. Place the plant materials directly on to the fabric. You can be quite random and playful, but try not to overload your fabric with different petals and leaves; we find using one plant stain sparingly helps create strong graphic patterns.

6. Spray it again with vinegar. Fold or roll your fabric into a tight bundle, then secure it using natural string or a rubber band.

7. Steam the bundle for an hour, rotating every 15 minutes for even colour dispersal (tongs are helpful as the fabric will be very hot). To do this, you can use a steamer tray in the pot, or create a makeshift steamer using a colander or sieve – again, make sure it's stainless steel and separate to your cooking equipment.

8. Remove the bundle from the steamer and leave it tied up in a warm place out of direct sunlight for at least 24 hours.

9. Unwrap your fabric to discover fantastic floral colours and patterns. Rinse the dyed fabric in lukewarm water thoroughly to remove any excess dye, then hand wash gently in a pH-neutral liquid soap. Dry and store away from direct sunlight.

Take your mind for a walk

IF YOU'RE FAILING to think clearly or find your natural flow, take a walk with no aim at all.

It's advice I've learned from Rose, who suggested a couple of years ago that we take a brisk stroll together before any important work meetings.

The workaholic in me would resist; I used to worry I didn't have time to leave my desk unless it was to walk my elderly border terrier, Huxley (who, by the way, liked to stand still a lot more than he liked to walk). I'd sit for hours engrossed but unproductive in my writing, forgetting to eat or drink and slowly withering while Rose would side-eye me, occasionally checking to see if I might need a glass of water.

She would tempt me out with a flask of her roasted dandelion root chai (we've shared this on page 140), and suggest we talk business on the walk, but of course we never did.

What she's taught me is that creative ideas are not conjured from thin air; great ideas are found and then cultivated. You can actually redefine your own notion of productivity and creativity by allowing yourself to do less, and tuning in to the world. This is when ideas will seemingly fall into your lap, almost heaven sent from the most mundane sources.

Sitting and ruminating only wastes time. As the writer Haruki Murakami says of his daily exercise, 'sometimes taking time is actually a shortcut'. When we feel overwhelmed, a walk around the block will often effortlessly present solutions. Walking without a goal is a sort of play – it opens our minds to discovery.

It's even been argued that walking can help us stretch time. We are comforted by routine, but can quickly lose focus when things become too familiar. By breaking out of the norm, scientists believe people's perception of time changes, because seeing unfamiliar sights helps us to create new memories.

'We gauge time by memorable events and fewer new things occur as we age to remember, making it seem like childhood lasted longer,' explains the neuroscientist Santosh Kesari. In this way, taking new routes and discovering new sights, sounds and smells on your walks might help you live seemingly longer days.

fail
to
grow

there

is no

right

way

REIGNITE

Stir your energies,
find a deeper peace

If there's one thing we want you to take from this chapter, it's that your senses are your superpowers – you just might not be tuning into their full potential.

And who can blame you? We know that the intensity of metropolitan life can be entrancing in short bursts, but without breaks the brain has to work hard to tune out the excess stimuli. Sometimes it's necessary to put blinkers on just to keep going. When nature's sights, aromas, tastes, sounds and textures do slink through the gaps, you might find you've forgotten how to properly engage.

Fortunately, the deep and primal part of ourselves knows better, and the time comes when it says: enough. You no longer want to feel distracted, with senses dulled. You long for a richer intimacy with your surroundings. You want to *really* feel again.

The good news is that to reconnect, you definitely don't need to abandon urban living. With fresh eyes and a better understanding of what you're tuning into, you'll find that nature's sensory gifts are not far from your doorstep, and they're waiting to stir your energy and help you to find a deeper peace.

These sensory experiences can also be easily introduced to your home to elevate your meals, living spaces and relaxation practices. By exploring the multisensory healing powers of nature, you can transform the way you engage with the world, no matter where you might be.

Once you get into the flow, you'll start seeking out new rituals and projects that tap into the power of your senses, using them to enrich your personal intentions – and that's when things become really interesting.

Everyday aromatherapy

MANY OF US who contracted Covid-19 lost our sense of smell and perhaps learned the term 'scent training' as therapy to reignite the nervous system of the nose. I was one of them and my sense of smell only fully returned when I was exploring this chapter, eight maddening months later. If you were one of those people whose noses went numb, I hope this chapter might help you, too.

Olfaction, or the sense of smell, is one of your most primal and evocative senses. Plants and trees release odours to attract pollinators and detract pests, but we associate their natural scents with so many sensations, from a sense of calm and safety to love and rejuvenation. Jasmine, juniper or eucalyptus might evoke happy memories of a grandparent's garden, freshly ground coffee beans might invigorate your mood, and the combination of woody clove and pine might send you straight back to Christmas day and that fluttery feeling you felt as a child.

The nerve that processes smell (the olfactory nerve) overlaps with the pathways in our brains that control memory, emotions and intuition. When a certain scent is present alongside a strong emotion, it's as if the two embalm and strengthen each other.

Organic scents reach us on a deep level, and connecting with them is a primal survival skill. They tell us whether foods are safe to eat, help us attract mates and alert us to our environment. Smell dictates flavour; when we taste something, we are actually experiencing a combination of smell, taste, texture and temperature. Incredibly, scientists think that we can remember as many as 50,000 unique odours and can detect up to a trillion.

On your next walk, stop and get close to evergreen leaves or the blossoms on trees to see what new sensory experiences they might offer. Get hands-on and rub leaves between your fingers to feel their texture and release fragrance, and even have a nibble if you know the plant is edible. The flavour and scent of food that's freshly harvested can't be beaten, so challenge yourself to grow one or two kitchen plants each month. It could be as simple as a nutritious sprouted microgreen (see page 164) or a perfumed herb like parsley or velvet-soft sage.

There isn't always the opportunity to stop and properly engage with scents outdoors, so grow a mini-sensory garden indoors and include rosemary and lavender to help recharge. They work brilliantly grown from plug plants (rather than from seed) and all you need is some free-draining compost and a sunny spot. They work brilliantly as companions in a window box.

Rosemary is linked to restoring smell and boosting memory. Lavender is believed to aid sleep, relaxation and mood. Each day, rub the tips of stems between your fingertips and inhale the essential oils. You could remind yourself of a memory that brings you pleasure, or think about a goal you'd like to achieve. You could even chew the herb for an added sensory spark.

Conjure mood with scent

SO HOW CAN you use the power of smell to enhance wellness? One way is to work out your intentions, choose a companion scent for each aim, then train your brain to combine the two.

Neuroplasticity (or brain plasticity) is the brain's ability to be malleable, to change and adapt as a result of experience. In the past it was believed that adult brains were rigid and incapable of growth, preventing profound changes in behaviour. Now, neuroscientists know that our brains are continuously 'pruning' and reinforcing neural pathways depending on how they are used. Science has shown it is absolutely possible to rewire parts of your brain by gaining new knowledge, experiences and memories.

And because scent has such a potent effect on the brain and our emotions, it is a mighty aid for this kind of mind training. It was fascinating to read the research of neuroscientist Dr Tara Swart, who believes we can consciously use smells to relax our nervous system and boost our mood. She also believes we can use scents to encourage good decision-making. Even something as simple as taking a bath with a scent you associate with security or homeliness, such as cinnamon, pine or lavender, can release the bonding hormone oxytocin and generate comfort.

We can use scents to master our emotions: they can ground, uplift, soothe grief and make us feel present. We can use them to set an intention for a space, for example a place in which we wish to be relaxed or creative. And by actively doing (or even visualising) a specific mood, and connecting it to a chosen smell, we can teach our brains to associate the two.

Revive your nose

If you find your sense of smell dampened, or want to forge a deeper connection to the scents you love, practise scent training. Choose three or four familiar smells (remember the ones that stir your emotions are the most powerful), and spend just 30 seconds each day focusing on breathing them in, one at a time. Over the course of a few weeks this will help stimulate your olfactory nerve and reignite neural pathways to supercharge their receptivity.

Our favourite fragrances for scent training are juniper, tomato leaves, fig leaves and sweet peas, but it's entirely personal, so explore your environment and search out new scents on your nature adventures. We like to blend a couple of our favourite essential oils in a small bottle to keep on our work desks – whenever we need a moment of peace, we take in a few deep breaths. Place it somewhere obvious so you'll spot it right in front of you as a reminder (see page 120).

Sink into

Soundscapes

the spit and pop of a glowing fire
surf washing a bay of shingle
a nightingale's evening melody
snapping crisp green beans
stochastic raindrops pattering on canvas
the groan of shifting glaciers
the hollow flute of a hooting owl
the aeolian rustle of a thousand leaves
a pine needle shower
softly crackling snow underfoot
rolling, rhythmic layers of chattering cicadas
the steady burble of a travelling river
distant undulating thunder
a moonlight chorus of croaking frogs
your body's rhythmic landscape

Heal with sound

Recharge by listening to nature sounds through headphones or speakers and create different moods in your living spaces. Everyone responds to different sounds: you might feel relaxed or even invigorated listening to lapping waves, cooing wood pigeons or a dramatic, stormy night.

Our favourites include choral bird song for relaxation, forest sounds for focus, a crackling fire for reading and rainfall for sleeping. If you prefer silence, but find yourself distracted by noisy neighbours or nagging thoughts, try listening to brown noise – it's a layered, deep frequency soundscape designed to muffle background noises. It sounds quite like a distant waterfall.

Use different daily soundscapes as an aid to boost relaxation. Take a few minutes to close your eyes and imagine your hearing is like a radar. Locate a sound as far away as possible, hold on to it for a few moments without needing to name or analyse it, and then let it go. Pick up another sound closer to you, and repeat, letting your ears scan the space around you. This is a really helpful way to practise meditation and you'll be surprised by how many layers of sound (both wild and manmade) you can connect to once you tune in.

A conversation with silence

HOW DOES THE word *silence* make you feel? Is it a luxury that you seek, or a sense of loss or nothingness? When we don't long for it, silence can seem lonely and unnerving, but when we befriend silence and learn how to explore the space within it, we can uncover a richness that helps us feel more connected.

In towns and cities, our brains register much of our auditory landscape as noise. We become so good at tuning unwanted sounds out that we eventually become deaf to the intricate melodies and rhythms of the natural world. 'The habit of suppressing sound,' says the soundscape designer Julian Treasure, 'has meant that our relationship with sound has become largely unconscious.' Listening has become a skill that we have to practise.

True silence is very rare; it's almost impossible to escape the beat and flow of the auditory landscape inside our bodies. It's the quieting of manmade sounds most of us long for, and when we make time to listen better, this can happen naturally. We find ourselves in a deeply attentive state, where the sonic beauty of nature takes over: chirrups, squawks, rustles, fluttering wings, crisp wind making dry leaves spin. For the sake of both precious urban wildlife and our own mental health, we must speak up and protest when we lose the option to shut out manmade noise.

In his book *Silence in the Age of Noise*, the explorer Erling Kagge explains how, if we allow it to, silence listens, and we can talk to it, whether we are alone or in company. 'Perhaps the most important thing we bring to another person is the silence in us,' he writes. 'Not the sort of silence that is filled with unspoken criticism or hard withdrawal. The sort of silence that is a place of refuge, of rest, of acceptance of someone as they are. Silence is a place of great power and healing.'

Silence is expansive, like still, open water or a clear blue sky. It's a spacious room of possibilities and discovery – a space we can fill with feeling. Avoid the temptation to take your phone or always invite a friend on your walks; being outside alone is a great opportunity to enjoy silence without the pressure to be sociable.

Delve into the mysterious whisperings of the northern lights, which were once thought to be silent. Search online for VLF (very low frequency) recordings capturing the Alaskan aurora borealis. Biologist Karin Lehmkuhl Bodony uses a device that turns radio waves given off by the sun's solar winds into soundwaves, creating an aural snapshot of the green-violet-pink electromagnetic light show. The VLF recordings sound like an ethereal duet between calling birds and cosmic chirping frogs, and somehow make you feel tiny yet completely melded with the universe.

Aromatherapy cleanses

NATURAL SCENTS HAVE the power to revive and relax, but you don't always need to be outdoors to appreciate them. Creating a homemade sensory spray or bath soak using ingredients from nature can cleanse your mood and conjure calming thoughts. Schedule a nature bath as a weekly treat, and use a spray during meditation or to help you unwind before bed.

You can even connect your bath soak or spray with your local environment – think about enriching your soak with fragrant flowers and herbs from your garden or window box, or foraging for ingredients in a nearby forest. We often use bladderwrack – a tendrilly jelly pod seaweed – that we forage from our local beach. When it is submerged in water, it releases nutrients that nourish skin.

The three scent blends we've included on the following pages are drawn from our experiences outdoors, but we invite you to experiment and create your own. Take a moment to recall a time with nature that you found healing – you might use a journal to make note of any smells or memories that come to mind (see page 22) – and then make a list of the essential oils you are drawn to and experiment with those.

Recipes for soaks and sprays

*Create a homemade aromatherapy bath soak or spray
using ingredients from nature*

1. YOUR EXPERIENCE	2. ESSENTIAL OILS SCENT BLEND	3. OPTIONAL EXTRAS	4. NATURE SOAK OR SPRAY
A breath of fresh air *Energy, Clarity, Positivity*	Cedarwood Eucalyptus Frankincense Peppermint Sweet fennel	Bladderwrack seaweed (for nature soak only)	NATURE SOAK
Back to the garden *Nostalgia, Relaxation*	Neroli Lavender Ylang ylang Rosemary Peppermint Dill	Dried or fresh rose or calendula flowers	NATURE SPRAY
After the rain *Grounding, Possibility*	Juniper berry Cypress Clary sage Sandalwood		

5. CHOOSE YOUR CARRIER OIL	6. ADD EXTRA MINERALS	7. METHOD	8. CARE
Olive Sesame Hemp Fractionated coconut Castor Jojoba MCT	Quartz crystal Himalayan salt Epsom salt Dead Sea salt	Fill your bath Combine 15ml (1 tbsp) of carrier oil with 15 drops of your chosen mix of essential oils. Add to the bath water Add a mineral of your choice and decorate with seaweed or flowers	After your nature soak, wash your bath with castille soap or baking soda to remove excess oils
Witch hazel water	Sea salt	Half fill a 120ml spray bottle with witch hazel water Add 60 drops of your chosen mix of essential oils and shake Top up with distilled water Test your spray and add more essential oils to reach the intensity you wish	Store in a cool, dark place

*Tune in to your
senses and ground yourself
in this moment.*

*To help you connect more
deeply with your surroundings,
press a finger on the dots one
by one and engage each sense.*

Right now I see

Right now I hear

Right now I smell

Right now I taste

Right now I feel

When you don't have this
book, press each of your
fingertips, one at a time, into
the palm of your other hand.

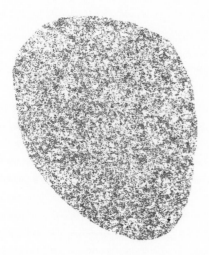

Work from your little finger
(right now I see) to your thumb
(right now I feel).

Go on, touch the calming blobs.

DISAPPEAR

You are small, but the possibilities are infinite

Any urban dweller lucky enough to care for even the tiniest scrap of garden or a balcony knows that a few stolen moments cocooned in daily gardening tasks can be the perfect way to disappear into green.

But many of us don't have this as an option, and besides, sometimes it's the less-familiar nature experiences – the ones that disorientate us and seem to return us to a more primal state – that we really crave and need.

The healing powers of lush forest walks, sea bathing and celestial stargazing may be easily found on the coast or in the countryside, but what about when those places are out of reach, when we don't have the time or funds to access those enchanting green portals that help us escape everyday life? Is it really possible to switch off from the hubbub without jumping on a plane, train or boat?

The key is to step out of your comfort zone and into the least familiar landscape you can access. Even in towns and cities there are immersive, all-encompassing experiences to seek out. When we find them, these are the places that epitomise the glorious spontaneity of urban life.

It takes a little self-persuasion and motivation: getting lost is something we're taught to be wary of as children. It's perhaps one of the reasons why, as busy adults, we seem programmed to choose the easy, fast and well-trodden course.

So the kinds of nature adventures we suggest over the following pages are perfect excuses to invite an equally footloose friend – tell them to keep the whole day free. These kinds of shared experiences can refresh our minds, help us to process emotions and provide us with some of our most joyful memories.

Shrink yourself and find awe

VISUALISE YOURSELF STANDING at the peak of a mountain taking in a vast landscape, diving into the beating sea or in a remote spot after darkness falls where the glittering cosmos overhead hints at its secrets.

Faced with nature on an epic scale, your worries can start to retreat. You are a tiny portion of the whole and at the same time infinite in your connectedness. In situations like these, we might experience the quieting of the ego and the silencing of the thinking mind, allowing the sensations of the physical body and spiritual self to ignite.

Grab a map and figure out the highest spot in your home town or city that you can access. That might mean puffing your way up the steepest hill of a park, cycling to a friend's house who has a roof terrace or reaching the top of a tall public building, like the viewing tower of the Blavatnik Building at Tate Modern in London, or Hudson Yards in New York. Ideally find a spot with an open-air observation deck so you can surrender to the elements and tune in to the sights and sounds around you without a sheet of glass in the way.

Your eyes are at their most relaxed when they rest on distant scenes rather than close-up details. When you arrive, take a moment to settle your sight on a distant skyline view. Let your eyes blur and release your focus. Feel your mind step away from some centre point and into the borders (that's where the best stuff happens). Allow yourself to accept things that are out of your control.

This act of surrender – this sensation that we are each a small part of something bigger and more intricate than ourselves – shows us perspective, humility and respect. It reminds us that all living things exist together. Experiencing awe is precisely the opposite of feeling anxious, despondent or trapped – it is the wonderful feeling of situating yourself in the context of the world around you, and it is feeling located.

Society tells us to be big and powerful, but when we grasp these rare moments to float above our home, we see what a release it is, actually, to simply be a drop in the ocean.

Urban birding

Tall urban buildings not only offer reviving panoramic views of uninterrupted sky, they also double up as surprisingly effective birdwatching towers, especially during migration seasons when hundreds of species – occasionally even rare ones – travel through cities.

If you can, take a full day off in the week and plan an urban expedition. Perhaps invite a friend to do the same. A midweek jaunt gives you the best chance of avoiding the crowds so you can tune in to the environment, make surprising nature observations, and generally take your sweet time. Pack a flask, sandwich, suncream and binoculars, and head out to walk a canal way, take a river swim, or find a tropical glasshouse to explore.

Bathe in green

YOUR BODY IS like a forest: sophisticated, beautiful and responsive to the environment in ways that can take a lifetime to discover. When you're feeling disconnected, there's no better way to reset than by going that little bit further to the borders of the city and diving into the lushest spots of green you can get to.

For those of us living in the concrete jungle, that might be a tropical glasshouse, a public garden, treasured park, woods or wetlands – these can be just as immersive and uplifting as a remote wilderness, sometimes even more so for their unexpected knack of merging nature with the manmade.

Not only has time spent walking in green been proved to boost people's calm and joy, it has been shown to improve attention, creativity and memory. It enhances cardiovascular function, regulates blood pressure and boosts energy levels. The mix of gentle exercise and mental health benefits even increases 'natural killer cells' – a type of white blood cell that plays a vital role in our immune system, reportedly fighting tumours and viruses. You'll even breathe healing scents in denser urban woodlands. Flora like pines and cypress emit protective essential oils called phytoncides that are said to strengthen our nervous system.

To get the most out of the experience, think about taking a step closer to all the flora and fauna that live in green. Get off the path and challenge yourself to connect with or identify the living things around you. You might come across enchanted oaks, puffball slime moulds, luminous moss and countless wildflowers.

Not to mention scampering, fluttering and wriggling things that add to the mix. In urban parks you'll sometimes find the especially frondy interrupted fern (*Osmunda claytoniana*) that has survived on Earth for millions of years, as well as hundreds of types of fungi like the edible sheathed woodtuft and turkey tail fungi.

Being in the presence of plants and animals can provide a jolt of optimism, their resourceful ability to thrive a reminder that we too are from nature and are strong and resilient.

To make the most of these experiences, gently encourage yourself to relax by not rushing through your walk. You might want to go alone (if you feel it's safe to) so that you can make the experience as mindful as possible.

Draw on your senses: notice vibrant flowers, the unique rustles and melodies of the creatures, the dull crunch of your footsteps as you abandon the trodden path and the earthy smells all around. Allow your hands to reach out to stroke the bark of trees and delicate leaves. Sit, if you can. Don't be embarrassed to take off your shoes and socks in the summer and indulge your feet in the textures underfoot. You'll be amazed by how liberating it feels.

It might sound strange, but cemeteries are often gloriously lush (and quite surreal) wedges of urban greenery to disappear into. They're usually tucked protectively within beautiful old walls and have become miniature ecosystems and valuable nature reserves because their largely undisturbed environments allow all kinds of flora and fauna to run riot, making use of sheltered spots and nesting nooks. They are wonderful examples of how well nature can adapt and survive in the city.

On your next expedition, collect a few foraged trinkets to adorn a shelf or windowsill. Look for dried seedheads, sea-worn flint, silky driftwood, a skeleton leaf, dried lichen or a patterned feather. Let these weathered souvenirs of distant landscapes bring tactile joy and evoke memories of faraway adventures whenever you're home and need inspiration. You could even arrange a composition of elements under magnified glass to form a surreal landscape.

Imaginary landscapes

MANY OF US experience restless nights, particularly when over-stimulation during the day can cause our natural sleep cycle to jitter out of sync.

Whenever you wake in the night feeling overwhelmed, try visualising a vast landscape to lose yourself in, where you are a tiny portion of the whole.

Draw inspiration from your most spiritual, immersive nature experiences. Perhaps it's the time you walked through a butterfly house, snorkelled in tropical waters, stood in an expanse of ochre desert or in the midst of dense woodland.

You might take a voyage of fantasy and visualise paddling a kayak along an estuary on a balmy day. Imagine being shielded on either side by mature trees and river reeds mirrored in azure water. Conjure the springtime melodies of chaffinches, nightingales, blackbirds and cuckoos, while gliding alongside water birds, like great-crested grebes, cormorants and white throated dippers. Keep your mind's eye on low-hanging branches where a beautiful kingfisher might be perched.

Build your own scene, then take a slow route through the landscape, allowing your mind to add details and immerse itself in place. It helps to embellish the scene with familiar flora that you are emotionally attached to, because your brain will unfurl the details without much effort.

We've had some of our most incredible nature experiences while visiting observatories, such as the Hampstead Scientific Society, which is tucked down a back street in north London, or the more famous Griffith Observatory in Los Angeles. With the help of a powerful telescope and a trained guide, you can recalibrate your perception of Earth by seeing just how enormous and beautiful the universe is – and how lucky we are to be floating in it.

Find out if there's an observatory you can reach fairly easily, and wait for a promising, clear-sky day to make a spontaneous trip with a friend. Observatories tend to be closed in the summer when evenings are light, so this is a brilliant chance to get a nature fix in autumn and winter – a dazzling dose of celestial awe will boost your mood and serve up a bit of seasonal magic.

FORAGED DRINKS TO QUENCH
A THIRST FOR ADVENTURE

ROASTED DANDELION ROOT CHAI

This sweet and spicy chai finds balance through cleansing dandelion root and is just the tonic to put a spring in your step. To roast your own foraged dandelion roots, thoroughly wash and remove the straggly parts of the root and upper green leaves. Cut the remaining chunky part of the root into 1cm rounds and roast on a tray in the oven for 40 minutes at 170°C.

1 tsp black peppercorns
5 whole cloves
4 green cardamom pods
1 whole star anise
Thumb-size piece of fresh
    ginger root, sliced into
    thin rounds
2 tbsp ground roasted
    dandelion root
500ml cold water
Dairy or plant milk of your
    choice
Raw honey or maple syrup

I. Lightly crush the dry spices using a pestle and mortar. Combine with the ginger and dandelion root and place in a saucepan with the water.

2. Simmer for 20–30 minutes.

3. Strain the liquid dandelion concentrate through a tea strainer or sieve into a sterilised jam jar.

4. In your insulated flask, combine 1 part dandelion concentrate to 2 parts hot or foamed milk and add honey or syrup to taste.

FIG LEAF COFFEE LATTE

This recipe is based on the stupendous cocktail our friend and chef Annie Nichols made at Rose's wedding. Aromatic coffee is infused with fig leaves, which are best harvested in spring and summer. The fig leaf syrup can be saved in a sealed, sterilised jar in the fridge for up to a year and used to sweeten a cocktail or drizzled on ice cream or pancakes.

500ml water
500g golden caster or
    coconut sugar
1 tsp vanilla extract
10 fig leaves, stems cut to the
    base of the leaf
Cold brew or espresso coffee
Dairy or plant milk of your
    choice

I. Combine the water, sugar and vanilla extract in a saucepan and place over a gentle heat until the sugar dissolves to create a syrup.

2. Cut the fig leaves into pieces and place in a bowl. Pour the syrup to cover them. Allow this to infuse for 30 minutes at room temperature. For a more intense flavour, leave for 24 hours in the fridge.

3. Strain the infused syrup into a large, sterilised jam jar to remove the leaves.

4. Part fill your flask with ice. Pour in 1 part coffee and 1 part milk. Add 1 tablespoon of infused syrup and shake. Add more syrup to taste.

Dissolve into water

IF YOU WANT to feel like you're being enveloped by nature, there's one thing we can't recommend enough: immersing yourself in wild waters. Urban bathing ponds, lakes and reservoirs are some of our most potent remedies for stress. Plunging into cold water gives the body an electrifying shot of endorphins: it's as if every nerve lights up and vibrates. It can improve your energy, circulation, libido and quality of sleep. Regular cold-water swimming is even believed to reduce inflammation and benefit the immune system.

Of course, city wildlife already appreciates the benefits of fresh water, so there's plenty of it to meet. Even if you're not in the water, you might spot Eurasian otters along city and town rivers (these are ever-more common), and maybe some seal pups basking in sunshine near estuary towpaths (we've spotted these cuties along the Thames). Slip into a bathing pond or lake and you'll be surrounded by (often quite surprised-looking) families of ducks, grebes, dragonflies and froglets.

The experience of silky, cool water embracing every crook and crease of your skin is alluring in its intense tactility. It's a full-body sensation that has the power to detach us from our anxieties and allows us to float in the bliss of physicality. Seasoned cold water swimmers speak of becoming hooked on the sense of aliveness it brings, of craving the unity between calm mind and body and seeking it out every day.

The idea might be out of your comfort zone. If so, all the more reason to try it: there's nothing quite so liberating. Choose a balmy day for your first dip – a flask of tea helps, too.

Lose yourself in a labyrinth

IN YOUR QUEST to embark on mindful adventures in your neighbourhood, it can be helpful to have a physical symbol which prompts you to focus your thoughts and transcend the everyday. A labyrinth is that symbol for us.

While a maze is designed to trick – with multiple paths and dead ends – a labyrinth offers just one meaningful, winding pathway into the centre and back out the same way, with no wrong turns.

For millennia the labyrinth has taken on various meanings and been used in its physical form in myriad ways. For some, walking a labyrinth was a way to make a remote pilgrimage, while others believed the symbol banished evil spirits. They've been used in rituals, religious and spiritual ceremonies, and even politics. We like the idea that a labyrinth's purpose is not to be challenging, frightening or confusing, but rather to facilitate a calm, spiritual journey to uncover inner peace and strength.

Around the world, the symbol crops up in different sizes and designs: mosaicked on Roman floors, painted in Indian temples, etched into ancient Cretan coins and the rock faces of mountains. The pattern has even been discovered inside prehistoric caves and tombs, presumably carved by long-forgotten people. More recent designs are often made from stone and turf, and found in forests and formal gardens.

For a modern-day pilgrimage, try playing with the concept of a labyrinth in your local park by creating your own. On your next visit, pick a point that feels special – it might be the spot with the best view, a pond or a tree you love. This is your labyrinth's central, pivotal point.

Next, track your eyes around the park's perimeter and choose an entrance point – the quieter the better. This will be both your entrance and exit from your labyrinth. Then all you have to do is to decide on the path you're going to take to the centre and picture it as a labyrinth – just make sure you take the same path back out.

You might use your labyrinth route to think over a personal issue, or simply walk meditatively, aware of your body and your beautiful surroundings. A labyrinth's route is intended to slow you down, so remember to take your time.

When you reach your pivotal point, stop for as long as you like and try to let any thoughts go. You might take some slow, deep breaths, acknowledging the journey you have made to get to this point. You might like to think of a future goal or intention.

Once you are ready, begin the same route out of the park in reverse. This is your passage back to reality, so allow yourself the same attention and time. Keep any future intentions in mind, tuning into the rhythm of your gait whenever your mind wanders. Notice how you feel as your final step releases you from your giant labyrinth.

Trace your finger slowly along the winding path of the labyrinth until you reach the centre. Take slow, deep breaths as you go. At the centre, hold your finger there, sit tall, close your eyes and take a few seconds or minutes to acknowledge where you are and how you feel right at this moment in time. See if you can feel gratitude for the present moment.

Flutter your eyelids open and let your finger follow the path back out. As you trace the path outwards, imagine your inner peace as something you can see and feel, then see if you can bring that inner peace to hug the space around you, breathing deeply as you do. Try to move slower than normal for the rest of the day, acknowledging and pausing on as many moments as you like.

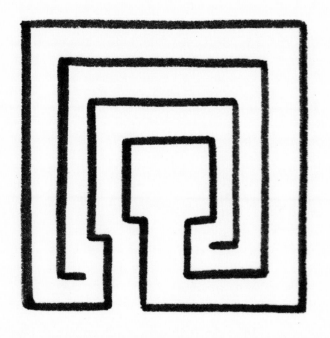

Try this sitting on a park bench.
We dare you.

RENEW

Value the old,
unearth truth

Something that has set me and Rose apart as indoor garden designers is our reputation for pushing large, elderly plants on our clients. Not literally (imagine the lawsuits). What I mean to say is that the brand-new plants grown en masse in sterile, controlled conditions just don't appeal to us; it's the old, rare, rebellious types that really animate a room.

They're healthier, too. Wonky and wizened does not necessarily mean faulty or unstable. Wonky is natural and resilient; old has narrative.

Nature has so much to teach us about renewal when we let it. The seasons, moon phases and life-cycles of animals (many that we can watch play out in the garden) all help demonstrate the value of cyclicity, while ancient woodlands, rock formations and the earth beneath our feet speak of ageing and adaptation.

Renewal is rarely about flashy change and big moves, but rather is about noticing, appreciating and encouraging new life, ideas and growth. To renew can be to rethink the way we look at something that might initially seem imperfect – it's an invigorating, grounding life skill.

In this chapter we'll share some ideas for how to tap into the mysterious qualities of ancient greenery, we'll use nature as inspiration to renew old things, and we'll also share the simple ways we have found to reduce and repurpose our waste.

We hope these suggestions will strengthen your desire for renewal and help you feel emboldened by change. By shifting your perspective on the magnetic quality of imperfection, you might refresh your vision, and may find yourself more aware of your own enduring qualities too.

Befriend an elderly giant

THERE IS AN ANCIENT hollow beech that I trek up to whenever I'm in Hampstead Heath in north London. It's tucked in a damp, sheltered patch of woodland, its branches sprawling resolute like a giant Louise Bourgeois spider.

Within the tree's gnarly trunk is a hollow space big enough to slip into, the inside polished smooth by the strokes of thousands of curious hands. I pat her trunk and remember the countless walks on the Heath that have helped me reaffirm my goals and bring focus to my desires.

Ancient trees are like grandparents – homely, stubborn and irreplaceable. And they're great listeners: they sit in one spot and lend their solidarity without any judgment or emotion. You can offload worries in their company and walk away feeling a little lighter.

Maybe they're time travellers. The most mature of our living trees seeded many hundreds of years ago, surviving countless challenges, human intervention and epic storms. Some cypress, yew, giant sequoia, African baobab, juniper, aspen, giant basin bristlecone pine and sweet chestnut have been known to live for thousands of years. Older deciduous trees like oaks, beech and maple will continue to seasonally shed and regenerate their foliage, like giant flowering plants.

Many urban trees were planted altruistically as saplings by people who would never see them in their grandeur, and then protected by those who knew they were destined to become the 'lungs' of expanding cities and towns and vital to our wellbeing. There's hope to be found in those strangers' acts of kindness.

You can tell an ancient tree by its very wide and sometimes hollowing trunk. Another clue is the vibrant wildlife you'll meet in their company. All manner of creatures depend on rotting wood for food and use the holes formed by damage and decay for nests and shelter: invertebrates like stag beetles and the goat moth, mammals like squirrels, birds like owls, parakeets and woodpeckers, as well as myriad microorganisms like mosses, fungi, lichens and liverworts. Revive your imagination by snooping around the various wonders you spot.

Look out for ancient trees in urban parks, cemeteries and gardens in the city, and in hedgerows and dense woodland further afield. They remind us to protect old things, not to avoid or be afraid of ageing, and to dive as deeply as possible into the human experience.

When gloomy winter days test your mood, remind yourself
of the spring that is sure to follow by visiting an ancient tree.
Stand or sit beneath its crooked arms, observing how they have
adapted to find light. Visualise the soles of your feet bridging
the soil and touching the tree's subterranean web of roots, right
down to the thread-like mycelial networks that allow mysterious
interconnectivity between trees. Breathe slowly and deeply in
the presence of one of your most powerful oxygen givers. Let it
bear witness to your feelings and refresh your spirit.

Look out for strays

YOU MIGHT FIND that your connection to a homeless plant – one you come across by accident – is fiercer than to one you actively seek out or buy.

Be it the wily, top-heavy succulent your friend desperately thrusts on you as you leave her house, a wilted basil plant on the supermarket 'reduced' shelf, the injured nasturtium you spot peeking out of a garden centre skip, or the baby Christmas tree you find in the bushes of your local park on new year's day, there's something about these hopeless creatures that tugs at our heartstrings.

I remember the day I moved house after a break-up, I discovered a sad-looking hare's foot fern discarded in a communal bin. Perhaps I was projecting how I was feeling – a bit lost and squashed – on to this abandoned thing, but I couldn't look away.

Ferns indoors normally make me nervous: my habit of living in a series of draughty flats has proved a death knell for feathery tropical species. Besides, it's a real downer when you manage to kill a plant that was resilient enough to survive an apocalyptic asteroid. But this one couldn't intimidate me. This one was already almost dead. And it was *old*. Judging by its mottled terracotta pot, it had lived a long and tough life.

For the next few weeks, I only had time for my adopted friend, and rolled my eyes at my other plants that showed signs of shock at the house move, tut-tutting as if they were spoilt children. I bustled about with tiny scissors and bought an ornate spray mister to boost humidity, desperate to give my fern a second chance at life.

And it thrived. Stray plants are a pleasure because they come with zero expectation, freeing you up to calm down and experiment. They inspire resilience and patience and maturity.

Stray plants are easier to come by than you'd imagine: keep your eyes peeled, and don't be afraid to roll up your sleeves to rescue them, then just watch as they become your favourites.

Root, nurture, grow

Plants that have been propagated from a friend's collection or passed along through the generations hold particular power. There's something comforting and connecting about growing a cutting from the salvia that's in your mum's garden and that was given to her by your gran. It's a pleasure to see a piece of the same plant blooming in both your own home and that of a sister or friend. These living gifts are a piece of home and a physical bond to our loved ones, past and present.

Ask a friend or relative if you can take a cutting from a plant you like the look of, one that seems healthy and vibrant. The best time to do this is usually spring and in the morning. Take a note of where it's growing – a sunny, sheltered spot, for example – and think about how you can recreate the same sort of conditions at home. The next growing season, continue the love by giving a little piece of it away to someone else, extending its magic even further.

Saving sickly houseplants

IF YOU COME across an abandoned houseplant that is brown and floppy, crispy, or generally looks sorry for itself, it's your chance to give it a new lease of life and welcome it into your plant family. You might come across a completely abandoned plant in the street (it's amazing how often people turn their back on ailing plants), or maybe you need to adopt a forgotten plant from a friend, colleague or neighbour.

However you find your poorly plant, first check its stems and roots for signs of life. Cut a stem and look for green, moist tissue inside. Next, check its roots, which should be pale and pliable, but not mushy. If you can't spot any obvious signs of pests or disease, the most likely cause of plant collapse is an extreme of one of its fundamental needs: temperature, water and light. (Though we recommend keeping it in isolation while you nurse it, just in case it is pests.)

Cut the plant right back to conserve its energy, pruning off all leaves and stems that are dead or sickly down to about 5cm above the soil, or to where you see healthy growth and new buds. Clean any healthy leaves of dust or grime. Feel the soil: if it's very dry all the way through to the bottom of the pot, give it a good soak. If it's sopping wet (even if it's just at the bottom), let it dry out before watering again.

Use filtered water or rainwater to avoid pouring in unnecessary chemicals that might push it over the edge. Hold off on fertilising for the moment as this might shock damaged roots. Place the plant in bright, indirect light away from fluctuating temperatures.

Once it grows back with some gusto, use a plant identifying app, book or online search to check the exact species and tailor your care to help it flourish. In spring, refresh the soil with a good-quality houseplant compost by carefully teasing away as much soil as possible without damaging the roots, and repotting with fresh compost. You ideally want the pot to be a few centimetres wider than the root mass on all sides.

Create a simple fertilising tonic for your houseplants by saving nutrient-rich water left over from draining boiled vegetables or eggs. The same goes for leftover brewed herbal tea leaves. Even old banana skins can be repurposed: leave them to soak in a bucket of water overnight to create a magical tonic to strengthen your plants during the growing season. Just make sure any hot water has cooled to room temperature before watering.

'I like the teacup
with a chip in it.
That's the one
with a story'

MATT HAIG

Diversify your view

A great way to renew your outlook and bridge the gap between you and the outdoor world is by becoming a citizen scientist.

Each year, various wildlife organisations and charities put out requests for the public to help them with their biodiversity and conservation research, setting up projects like the RSPB's Breakfast Birdwatch or Butterfly Conservation's Big Butterfly Count. You might be asked to note down the number of butterflies and daytime moths you encounter in a day, record the signs of spring from your window, list the birds you spot during your breakfast cup of tea, or identify mosses in your garden.

During each project or count, you could also log anything you encounter in your journal, perhaps adding a quick sketch or observation. If you're worried you don't know how to identify the wildlife you meet, there are various apps and books that can help identify that mystery flower in the neighbour's front garden or the bug wiggling its antenna on the park bench next to you. You never know, you might find you've spotted something really rare.

Garden microgreens

DOES STARTING YOUR own vegetable patch feel like a faraway fantasy? For the longest time Rose and I didn't have the space or resources to do anything other than dream about harvesting our own food from the earth. We found that growing microgreens offered us a way to cultivate edibles on a small scale, whatever the weather and no matter where we were living.

Microgreens are nutrient-dense seedlings grown to be harvested in the early stage of the growth, and all sorts of seeds like cauliflower, red cabbage, broccoli, rainbow chard, radish, coriander and sunflower (the list goes on) work really well. If you give it a go, we'd suggest you find your feet with the forgiving mustard family: rocket, radish or mizuna. Recycled fruit, vegetable and salad plastic containers make the perfect miniature greenhouse and you don't need much compost.

Overseeing the seeds bursting and unfurling into a tiny forest of vibrant green stems is a marvel to watch. From two weeks after planting, use snips to harvest juicy stems just above the soil, eating them straightaway to hold on to valuable nutrients. Microgreens range in flavour from nutty and peppery to tangy citrus. Use them in smoothies or salads and to garnish just about anything.

GROW YOUR OWN
GARDEN MICROGREENS

FIND YOURSELF:
—— Spray bottle
—— Plastic vegetable punnets with drainage holes
—— Bowl
—— Kitchen paper
—— Organic peat-free seed compost
—— Seeds (ideally organic/fungicide free)

EXTRAS FOR THE MICRO-GARDEN AFICIONADO:
—— T5 grow light or daylight bulb

1. Add the soil to a bowl and moisten with water: think damp and slightly sticky, rather than sodden.

2. Line each tray with a sheet of kitchen towel to stop water from draining straight through when watering. Fill with about 3cm of the damp soil and gently tamp it down for an even surface.

3. Scatter the seeds more densely than the packet suggests so you get a full micro-forest. Gently press them into the soil, and for smaller seeds, cover with a thin layer of soil. Lightly water with a spray bottle.

4. Find a spot away from radiators or draughty windows, ideally a warm, bright place that's not in harsh sunlight.

5. Cover the tray with a damp paper towel and mist it daily so it stays moist. Within 3–5 days you will see your seeds begin to germinate. Remove the paper towel and place the uncovered tray on a bright windowsill.

6. Water the seedlings from the top using a spray bottle or place your tray on top of a watertight tray and water from the bottom.

7. Harvest your microgreens when they are between 3–7cm tall, depending on the variety. Microgreens are best when the seedlings have their first true leaves (ones that resemble the leaves of the fully-grown plant). Eat them fresh for a nutrient hit.

Savour precious seeds from your organic food waste that would otherwise end up in the bin or compost heap. Collect seeds from fresh chillies, mangoes, dates, citrus fruits and lychees. You can even sprout whole sweet potatoes by simply sitting them in a glass of water.

Pretty much everything in life encourages us to see time as a linear construct: on we march, hooked on schedules and deadlines and at the mercy of the ticking clock. But nature's cyclical forms and rhythms — the seasons, the lunar calendar, the reassuring life-cycles of creatures little and large — can remind us that we are part of an expansive, more rounded whole.

Sunset and sunrise are some of the greatest (and easy-to-witness) examples of circular time. These pivotal daily moments can transform your mood and renew your energy, gratitude and sense of oneness with the world.

Choose a date to catch either the sun rise or set, and commit to the ritual with a mark in your diary. If you're not an early riser, challenge yourself to a sunrise and notice how the experience shapes your day.

You could invite someone to join you in this shared joy, and head out together to experience it from a local vantage point, or simply open the front door and see what you can see. As the show of light unfolds, bask in the sun's glow and visualise the chromatic beams of sunlight connecting your heart to the sky, forming a golden, halcyon bond.

SHARE

Open up, find freedom

For me and Rose, the quest for green hasn't been purely a personal one. We've forged our daily outdoor rituals and found release and escape in the outdoors, but that personal process has also encouraged us to look beyond our own connection to nature and fuelled a fire to reignite all kinds of lost connections.

Plants are so universally cherished that they offer us a tangible way to bridge divides and express affection. Anyone who has carried a leafy green friend home on public transport knows that, much like having a dog by your side, a plant is like kindling, sparking spontaneous smiles and chats with strangers. There's some kind of enchantment inside seeds, roots, buds – these physical manifestations of hope – that bond us together.

And that's what's on offer when we share in the wonders of green. It could be finding common ground with neighbours. It could be about uniting to protect the precious patches of green in our towns and ensuring a future we can rely on.

At the right moment, one gifted seedling or invitation to go on an outdoor adventure can cause a ripple of positivity that might nudge someone to share more deeply with you, perhaps even sparking the beginning of their own journey into green. Surprise someone with a woody cherry tree cutting or handful of fresh figs, and juicy stories are sure to follow.

Working with plants has taught us to expect almost immediate openness and connection with the people we cross paths with. Our mutual love of the planet opens up all sorts of possibilities: community, kindness, spaces to listen and be heard. Because isn't that what we're hoping for, really? A stronger sense of kinship?

We flourish together

I'LL NEVER FORGET the day we launched our market stall, which was about a year before east London's houseplant mania really took hold. Word spread like bindweed: there were *really tiny* cacti for sale. Soon-to-be plant parents descended in swarms, cooing adoringly, and by lunchtime every prickly pup on our stall had a new home. Those people kept coming back, and they brought their friends, who came back too.

We'd never known kinship like it. We would set up shop every Saturday from 8am – teeth chattering through winter – and all day the friendliest people would introduce themselves and share their botanical stories, advice and questions. Sure, it was the miniature succulents in their impossibly cute terracotta pots that they came for, but we basked in our plants' greenish glow, establishing countless friendships and connections.

Whether it's through a bona fide plant society, green-fingered WhatsApp group or simply a crowd of self-confessed houseplant addicts huddling around a market stall, indoor gardening communities are so welcoming because we all want to see each other (and the plants) succeed.

Softening the edges of our interior spaces with lively palms, golden terracotta and creeping vines helps us feel grounded, and gives us a sense of belonging. Many of us rent our homes or don't have access to a garden, so houseplanting feels celebratory, a creative way to personalise our surroundings – no houseplant enthusiast we've ever met is bothered about competition or taxonomy.

Instead, we share cultivation advice and intel on how to track down that coveted species of monkey's tail cactus or monstera. We swap propagation advice, and maybe later, peperomia and strawberry begonia babies.

If you'd like to find a new tribe to share your houseplant hobby with, a great place to start is your friends and colleagues. Let people know that you're cultivating a green oasis at home, share your intentions and ask if they might want to create a green space too. Start a small group chat to share your plans and victories. Creating a mini-community to grow with will boost your motivation, naturally nudging you to keep at it until cultivating plants becomes part of your daily life.

If your pals don't share your hobby (give them time), see if you can find a local houseplant society to join. But for the sake of building a better sense of local community, preventing the spread of plant disease and reducing air miles on any plant swapping, see if there are societies or clubs near you first. Make friends with local plant shop owners and ask if you can help them organise a propagation party.

If you can't find anything near you, start your own group, and shout about it online; you'll be amazed how many people in your area will crop up and be eager to build new relationships.

If you're struggling to get going with a project, a garden, an *anything*, try planting seeds, bulbs or plug plants in a pot to give as a gift. Removing yourself from the end goal, and doing something in the service of others, might inadvertently give you the nudge you need to set off on a new path.

No matter the season, carry some garden scissors and bring the outdoors inside to share in its transient beauty. This might be pine cones in autumn, a delicate blossom stem in a vase in spring, a riot of wildflowers in a jam jar in summer or foraged firs, chives, eucalyptus and heather for a dried wreath in winter.

New roots in community

WE ARE YET to meet a gardener who hasn't wanted to share their time, their knowledge or their crop. We suspect that people who spend most of their days outdoors must be gifted with a particularly special energy.

Learning from these experienced gardeners is one of the best ways to nurture your own fledgling passion – and spend a few more hours outdoors yourself. Plus, it can be daunting to commit to a flower or veg patch alone, with only the vast online world to ask for help, so seeking likeminded people as you embark on your adventure will only keep you motivated.

To find your feet, look for community or therapeutic gardens near where you live. Though most aren't open to the general public, they are invariably underfunded and very much appreciate the offer of voluntary help. Turn up in clothes you don't mind getting messy in and you'll likely find yourself learning on the job, knee-deep in a potato trench before you've even explained why you're there. If you have no gardening experience at all, you could donate a useful item or an entirely different skill (such as advice on marketing or IT support) in exchange for some basic hands-on training.

If you can't find a welcoming green space to join, rally a group of three or four friends who live close by and make some united goals. If one of you has a communal garden, be bold and ask the landlord if you can add some charm with a flower patch or raised bed. If not, you might make friends via letter with an elderly neighbour and suggest you get creative in their garden in exchange for a bit of company or some help with weeding.

Once you have the spot secured, save funds and reach out to people by asking others in your network if you can borrow tools and any surplus materials like timber or soil in exchange for some of your harvest. Autumn and winter are the best seasons to start planning and clearing a plot, and any time from late winter to early spring is a good time to start sowing seeds and growing.

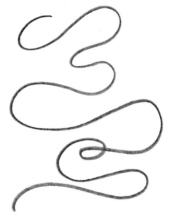

A small plot for fresh veg

1. Lettuce 15 x 15cm	5. Bush courgette 80 x 80cm	*Plan your plot using these*
2. Lavender 20 x 20cm	6. Compact squash 80 x 80cm	*spacings. Plant the*
3. Chives 15 x 15cm	7. Basil 20 x 20cm	*basil and lavender around*
4. Swiss chard 20 x 20cm	8. Bush tomato plant 40 x 40cm	*the borders to deter pests*

FOR BOTH:

For around 10–20 plants, build a bed of roughly 90cm x 190cm with a depth of no less than 50cm. Add a mix of 50:50 compost and organic, enriched topsoil for fertility. Apply an organic liquid fertiliser once a month in the growing season.

Spring & summer blooms for bouquets

1. Cosmos 'Cosmic Orange' 30 x 30cm
2. Clary sage 30 x 30cm
3. Foxgloves 40 x 40cm
4. Delphinium 'Magic Fountain' 50 x 50cm

5. Dahlia (dwarf bedding type) 30 x 30cm
6. Poppy anemones 10 x 10cm

Plan your plot using these spacings and tuck trailing nasturtiums into small corners to deter pests

FOR BOTH:

Germinate seeds indoors during spring, then transplant the seedlings to your raised bed once the risk of frost has passed – this helps protect plants from slugs and pests while they establish themselves.

Find a New

ditch your phone
organise a plant swap at work
root a few extra cuttings to give away
add pots and hanging baskets to communal doorsteps
donate surplus plants to a local school or nursing home
raise someone's spirits with a pot of daffodils
give your free time to a community garden
tell a plant's story when you give a piece of it away
adopt a Kalanchoe baby and become a mother of thousands
divide a fern into three and give a piece to your bestie...

Flow

...and another to a stranger

search for community seed swaps

help a neighbour with their garden in exchange for cuttings

buy soil in bulk and share with neighbours

gift a rootless air plant to someone who's moving away

offset sibling strife with Echeveria babies

trade your objects or skills for green things

thank your therapist with the weirdest cactus you can find

let it go

let go

Marvellous seed dispersion tactics

1.

2.

3.

1. WIND
Ash, sycamore, field maple

For the spontaneous: trust in fate, you
never know where you'll land next

2. HOOKS
Burdock

For the inexperienced: find someone
who's already doing it, cling on to
them and learn their tricks

3. ANIMALS
Orange

For the curious: absorb as much
information as possible and
see where it takes you

4. SHAKING
Poppy
For the active: be the mover,
the shaker, the action embracer

5. GRAVITY
Horse chestnut
For the grounded: trust your intuition,
staying close to your roots can be
powerfully effective

6. EXPLODING
Squirting cucumber
For the excitable: shout about your
plans and be bold with it

4.

5.

6.

Be like a seed and embrace unconventional
ways to spread your roots and find your
happy place.

Guerrilla gardening

A PLOT OF your own to sow seeds can be hard to come by. If you find that there are no available community growing spaces in your area and no chance of a garden or balcony, take inspiration from guerrilla and nomadic gardeners, and search out a patch of derelict land to beautify.

Throughout the history of our expanding cities – from the suburbs of Glasgow to inner-city New York – people have gardened on disused public and private land, be it a rooftop, vacant parking space or kerbside scrap of grass. Urban farming has become a recognised way for residents to regenerate their neighbourhoods and take back some control.

You might have heard of Ron Finley, the so-called Gangsta Gardener who has worked for more than a decade in his area of Los Angeles – despite strong resistance from local authorities – to empower his community to grow food on public land. He believes, and has proved, that growing your own food (and having access to green space and fresh produce) boosts health and uplifts wellbeing. (For the full story, there's a link to his TED talk on urban farming on page 190.)

The message these guerrilla gardeners pass forward is that growing plants in public spaces empowers you and your community – it's a way to cultivate hope through beauty, and power through food and nourishment.

Find some allies and together identify a patch of wasteland in your local area. Make sure to research whether it's public land or privately owned, and ask for permission to grow on it. Emphasise that your plans are to beautify the land and to build a sense of community. If you don't get a response, start planting anyway, and update the landowner or council with your progress.

Whether your patch becomes an established and permanent garden, or acts as a temporary link between people and land, you are sure to counter the feelings of isolation and transience that many urban neighbourhoods struggle with. Bringing nature into a formerly neglected plot and creating a positive space for your community… well, what could be more powerful than that?

'To change the community, you have to change the composition of the soil. We are the soil'

RON FINLEY

Further reading

Caro Langton & Rose Ray
*House of Plants: Living with
Succulents, Air Plants and Cacti*

Caro Langton & Rose Ray
*Root Nurture Grow:
The Essential Guide to
Propagating and Sharing
Houseplants*

Bloom
www.bloommag.co.uk

Maria Popova
Brainpickings
www.brainpickings.org

Ron Finley
www.ted.com/talks/ron_
finley_a_guerrilla_gardener_
in_south_central_la

Rob Walker
*The Art of Noticing:
131 Ways to Spark Creativity,
Find Inspiration, and Discover
Joy in the Everyday*

Sue Stuart-Smith
*The Well Gardened Mind:
Rediscovering Nature in the
Modern World*

Austin Kleon
*Keep Going: 10 Ways
to Stay Creative in Good
Times and Bad*

Sarah Kate Benjamin
and Summer Singletary
The Kosmic Kitchen Cookbook

Ula Maria
*Green: Simple Ideas for
Small Outdoor Spaces*

Isabel Hardman
*The Natural Health Service:
What the Great Outdoors
Can Do for Your Mind*

Isabella Tree
*Wilding: The Return of
Nature to a British Farm*

Acknowledgements

Mountains of gratitude to our agent Laura McNeill, editor Zena Alkayat, Hannah Dussold and our publishers Frances Lincoln and Andrews McMeel for believing in this book and for all your positive and illuminating instruction. Also to illustrator Georgie McAusland and designer Giulia Garbin for bringing our ideas to life so beautifully.

Thank you Claire Ratinon for writing 'Start a Garden' and for her guidance with the raised bed designs. And to Andrew O'Brien, Georgina Reid, Jane Perrone and Lindsay Sekulowicz for their short stories – so good, in fact, we have held them back for another book.

Thank you Lily Buchanan and Angela Tye for their advice and drawing tips, Helen Burley for the fabric dyeing expertise, Reebs Muncini for her meditation lessons, Annie Nichols for inspiring the seasonal drinks recipes, and Alice Vincent for the brilliant wildflower balls tip.

Special gratitude to Mark Brown for the invigorating chats, endless meals and for letting us steal all his best books. And to Petor Georgallou for inspiring outdoor adventures. A huge thank you to our friends for their continued support, and to our beloved parents for giving us an open, green introduction to life.

Caro & Rose

First published in 2021 by Frances Lincoln
an imprint of The Quarto Group.
The Old Brewery, 6 Blundell Street,
London, N7 9BH, United Kingdom
www.QuartoKnows.com

bloom
gardening · nature · inspiration

A Bloom book for Frances Lincoln
www.bloommag.co.uk

A catalogue record for this book is available from the British Library.

ISBN 978-0-7112-6681-0
978-0-7112-6976-7

Design by Giulia Garbin

Printed in China

FSC
www.fsc.org

MIX
Paper from
responsible sources
FSC® C016973